Dennis C Stevenson Jr

www.dennis-stevenson.com

Copyright © 2020

All rights reserved.

Cover ©
GermanCreation

ISBN: 9798675178117

STUDY THE BIBLE
Six Easy Steps WORKBOOK

2

Lesson Plan

01 **What is the Bible?** How you view the Bible dictates how you study it

02 **Choosing the right kind of study** There are many different ways to study the Bible.

03 **Foundations of Textual Study (1)** Tools to help you understand what the passage is trying to say

04 **Foundations of Textual Study (2)** Understand how words impact the meaning of the passage

05 **Applying what you learn** The study is incomplete until you apply it to your life

06 **Using resources wisely** Choosing the right resource can make a difference in your study

07 **Introduction to Titus** Get prepared for your first Bible study

08 **Titus Chapter 1** Digging into God's word, one chapter at a time.

09 **Titus Chapter 2** A deeper look at Titus chapter two

10 **Titus Chapter 3** Finishing up Titus by studying chapter three

Introduction

About this Study Guide

Studying the Bible is a core activity of the healthy Christian life.

From the earliest days of the church, the model has been for Christians do dig into God's Word to understand how to live their lives (Acts 17:10-11).

Scripture itself is identified as the final source for establishing right thinking, exposing error, applying correction and instructing the believer in right living (2 Timothy 3:16).

Despite the scriptural imperative, most adult Christians have not been taught the fundamentals of how to study the Bible.

This six week course , intended for normal believers, will introduce you to the basic skills needed to study the bible. It lays a foundation of knowledge which can be expanded later with more in-depth levels of study.

01
What is the Bible?

How you view the Bible dictates how you study it

01 What is the Bible?

How we view the Bible drives how we study it

How would you read the Bible if it were ...

A Newspaper

_____

_____

A Novel

_____

_____

A Textbook

_____

_____

A Fortune Cookie

_____

_____

Everyone has an opinion about the Bible.

We all think of it in a specific way. Perhaps it's something that was modeled for us when we were younger or impressionable. Maybe it's something that we picked up from our peers or those around us. It could be that we pieced together our thoughts about the Bible from bits and snatches at church. For some, we have no idea what to think about the Bible and just make it up as we go along.

These opinions we bring with us are not free. In fact they have a real impact on how we view the Bible and what we expect from it. From instilling reverence to determining what we choose to read to impacting how we understand it, our opinions are vitally important.

Before we begin we need to look at these opinions about the Bible.

The Bible is communication from God

Psalm 119:11 – By knowing God's word (memorizing it), we are able to avoid sinning and live a life pleasing to God.

Psalm 119:105 – God's word provides direction and instruction for living.

Proverbs 30:5 – God's word is pure and untainted. It serves as a shield for those who trust in God.

John 6:67-68 – Peter recognized that what Jesus was saying was different than everyone else and the key to life (eternal).

Acts 6:7 – When the Word of God increased (was presented more boldly, more often), the church grew.

Hebrews 4:12 – The word of God has power and effect in our lives.

Traditionally we say "the Bible is the Word of God."

This statement is foundational to our understanding of the Bible and defines it's priority in Bible study.

In everyday conversation we use words to communicate to each other. God chose to use the same communication, and expressed Himself in words – which we have today as the Bible.

God is the author of the Bible

The Bible was "breathed out" by God through human hands.

2 Peter 1:19-21 - The Holy Spirit was the motive force in its creation.

2 Timothy 3:16 - God breathed, profitable to define truth, identify error, correct wrong thinking, leading back to the right path.

Even though as many as 39 individual people are attributed as having written books, God is the ultimate author. The verses in 2 Peter and 2 Timothy make it very clear that God was present in the writing. "men spoke from God as they were carried along by the Holy Spirit." Here we see 2 members of the trinity involved in the writing of the scriptures.

The beauty of God's authorship of the Bible is that He allowed the individual people to express His message in their own voice, using their own unique style and words. Read a passage in the gospel of John and compare it to a passage in Hebrews, 1 Corinthians or Isaiah. They all sound very different. That's because different people were involved with God to put the words down.

Because God is the ultimate author, we see, through study, that the Bible is consistent and has one clear message that flows from Genesis to Revelation.

We find no error in the Bible

Doctrine of Inerrancy:

The teaching that the Bible is without error.

A doctrine is a teaching that is held to be true, often the foundation of a system of belief or faith.

The Bible is inerrant

Inerrant means "without error". Since the Bible is the Word of God, it carries the character and nature of God (God cannot speak contrary to His nature). Since God is true, complete, and trustworthy, His Word bears these same distinctions.

ALL of the Bible is inerrant – it does not "contain" the Word of God, it IS the Word of God. If some of it is not trustworthy, then none of it can be trustworthy and all of it is under a cloud of doubt.

Inerrancy applies to the original writing of the Bible. These originals have been, through the providence of God, carefully copied and maintained. They give us the manuscripts we have today, which are the basis of our English translations.

The Bible is our authority

Everywhere and every time the Bible speaks, it speaks with the words and voice of God.

What the Bible says is God saying it. Since God is the author, and is in control of what the Bible says, we give the words of the Bible the same weight and authority as if God sat down with us and said the words directly to us.

There is no authority over God (Romans 13:1). He is the ultimate authority, and is above every other authority that we will encounter or can imagine. All authority flows from God, and His word is the voice of that authority.

Everything the Bible says is with the authority of God!

What is our proper relationship to the Bible?

Psalm 1:1-2 - The Old Testament extols the person who lives by obeying the Word of God

2 Timothy 2:15 – Our right relationship is to study God's word – so that we handle it rightly

If you want to hear God speak to you, read your Bible. If you want to hear God speak audibly, read out loud!

Meaning & communication

The purpose of communication is to deliver a specific message from a sender (speaker) to a receiver (listener or reader).

The message is determined by the sender. It is not appropriate for the receiver to try to determine the message.

Any deviation from the sender's intention in the receiver's understanding is called "miscommunication".

The Bible is God's Word to us; therefore it has a specific meaning.

2 Peter 1:16-21 – The Bible has no private interpretation (hidden meanings, custom messages)

Each passage has one meaning, although it may have several implications (these are not the meaning), and many applications.

What it means "to me"

It's common and familiar to talk about what the Bible means "to me". As a student of the Bible, this is not a proper approach. God says the same words to everyone, with the same meaning.

The message of the Bible is the message. Period. How a person chooses to apply that message varies from person to person. But the meaning remains the same for everyone.

The Bible impacts your life right now!

It is not enough to know the truth about the Bible. In order for the truth to have any impact, it must affect the way I live my life. The impact of the truth is directly proportional to how much it affects me and the way I live.

Do you show respect to your Bible that matches your reverence for its contents?

_____

How often do you read the Bible? Is it enough?

_____

_____

Do you understand what it says; are you striving to go deeper?

_____

_____

In what areas of your life do you need to begin to obey what you read in the bible?

_____

_____

02
Choosing the right kind of study

There are many ways to study the Bible.

02 Choosing the right kind of study

Bible study is for everyone!

Most believers want to study the bible, but have no specific idea of what that means or how to go about it.

Christian bookstores are full of books about "Bible Study" and even provide Bible study tools. But the average person is more confused by the options than clarified. Where to begin? Which method to pick? What is the "best study" available?

In church believers might hear about others who are studying the Bible. It could seem complicated or scholarly. They might even conclude that since they haven't gone to Bible School, they don't have the skills to study the Bible.

The truth of the matter is that there are many different methods of studying the Bible. Some are so simple that anyone could do it. Others are more complicated and would benefit from instruction or specific training.

The bottom line is that no believer should ever be excluded from studying the Bible. In writing to his partner Timothy, the Apostle Paul says "study to show yourself approved." He doesn't put any restrictions or limits on it. Just study. Do what you can with the skills you have!

This lesson focuses on understanding different kinds of Bible study – and you will be able to start with at least one of them today.

Different Bible studies for different reasons

Not all types of study are created equal.

Not all types of study are appropriate for every situation or circumstance. For the believer, understanding the types of study and appropriate use is critical to spiritual development.

Some types of study are better suited for beginners and other types are better suited toward more mature believers. But that doesn't change the fact that studying the Bible is right for <u>all</u> believers. No one gets an excuse not to study the Bible.

The key for you is to begin with the kind of study which is best suited to your level of maturity and skill. Then progress from there. In a year, or 5 years time, you should want to be ready for more in-depth study. That is the natural path of development. – from the simple to the more mature.

Milk vs. Meat

Hebrews 5:12-14 – The writer expected that at this time the readers should be mature and able to handle spiritual "meat". Instead they were immature and could only handle spiritual "milk".

1 Corinthians 3:2-3 – Paul gave the Corinthians basic., or "milk," level teaching because that was all they were able to handle.

Study for the right reasons

2 Timothy 2:25

Do your best to present yourself to God as one approved, a worker who has no need to be ashamed, rightly handling the word of truth.

It is vitally important that when you study the Bible, you do so for the right reasons. Studying is not a badge of honor or status. It does not earn you points with God. The King James bible translates "do your best" as the word "study" and suggests the idea of preparing for a test or an exam.

Paul describes the life of study as a desire to please God. It is the way to live a life that results in the divine pronouncement "Well done, good and faithful servant!" This is a life of which God approves. One that is conformed to His values and demonstrates the fruit of the Spirit (Galatians 5:22-23).

For the Christian who studies and understands what God wants and expects of him or her, there is no shame. Paul suggests that there will be some Christians who will stand before God and leave ashamed that they didn't please Him more. These will be the Christians who did not do their best.

Different types of Bible study

The remainder of this lesson will look at the different types of study which are available to the Christian. You can see from the list to the right that there are many different options available.

From this list, you will undoubtedly be able to find one or more options which will be suitable to you in your walk with Christ. What's more, this list should also challenge you to grow and be able to take on more and different types of study.

Our goal as believers is to continually progress from a simple (milk) understanding to a more mature (meat) understanding of God's word.

Memorization

Meditation

Reading

Textual Study

Topical Study

Systematic Study

Memorization

Psalm 119:11

I have stored up your word in my heart, that I might not sin against you.

The simplest kind of studying the bible is memorizing it. The Psalmist says it best... I have memorized God's word so that I will not sin against God. Knowing what God expects is the first step to pleasing Him.

By memorizing God's word, I guarantee that I have it with me wherever I go. This means that whatever my circumstances, I can connect with what God has said:

- When I am tempted to sin – God's word will point out the right path
- When I need encouragement, I remember who God is and what He has already done.
- When I need to be reminded of who I am in Christ, I can focus on what God says
- When I need to know the right thing to do, God's wisdom can be brought to mind

Memorization works best with scripture that has clear meaning. It does not provide any real mechanism to understand more complicated passages. The point of memorization is to bring God's word to mind and focus on what He has said.

Biblical Meditation

Biblical meditation is about filling your mind with God's word.

Biblical meditation is simply thinking about, concentrating on, considering and pondering God's word. Typically it begins with a relatively short segment of scripture that is brought to mind. The best passages are often those which are image-oriented, or which have a clear message.

Biblical meditation works very well in conjunction with memorization. This makes meditation mobile. However you can also meditate on a passage of scripture that you have just read (but not yet memorized).

The point of Biblical meditation is going over the scripture again and again. The word picture is similar to that of a cow chewing it's cud. Just when you think you're done, go over it again... and again!

Joshua 1:8
This Book of the Law shall not depart from your mouth, but you shall meditate on it day and night, so that you may be careful to do according to all that is written in it. For then you will make your way prosperous, and then you will have good success.

Philippians 4:8 Finally, brothers, whatever is true, whatever is honorable, whatever is just, whatever is pure, whatever is lovely, whatever is commendable, if there is any excellence, if there is anything worthy of praise, think about these things.

Bible Reading

Through the Bible in a year

Chronological Bible

Through the NT in a year

Psalms & Gospels

Proverb a Day

Accelerated plans

Bible reading is a simple form of the next type of study we will consider: Textual Study. But it is a common, and valuable study tool for the believer.

The point of reading the Bible is to understand what it has to say. Let's face it, if we don't know what God has said in the Bible, we will have a very difficult time doing what it says.

The key to reading the Bible is to have a plan. There are lots of plans available that could provide structure and guidance to your Bible reading time. Pick one, based on what might interest you, or how much time you might have. The entire Bible can be read aloud in about 75 hours. So it's much more accessible than you might think.

As you are reading the Bible, remember, these are God's words for you. Pay attention and listen to what they have to say.

Textual Study

Textual study is the foundational process to learn and apply God's truth to my life.

The purpose of this study method is to understand what God's word communicates to people (in general) and me (in particular). This is probably what most people think of when they hear the phrase "study the Bible".

In general, textual study follows this pattern:

- What does the text mean (original author to audience)?
- How does it apply to me (general vs. personal)?
- What must (should) I do?

Subsequent lessons will dive into how to pursue this method.

Textual study is critical for the "right handling of the Word of God." (2 Timothy 2:15) It focuses on understanding what God has said. Italso demands application in our lives.

In 2 Timothy 3:14-17, the Apostle Paul describes the impact of scripture in the life of his protégé Timothy. Paul says that from Timothy's earliest days the scripture was preparing him for salvation. Now that he is saved, scripture has the effect of teaching truth, exposing error and providing correction back to the right path.

The goal of studying scripture is that the man or woman of God is complete, lacking nothing, and prepared for every good work.

Topical Study

Topical study is similar to textual study in many ways. It is primarily interested in understanding what God's word has to say. However instead of focusing on a specific passage or section of scripture, it picks a word or a topic and considers it throughout all of scripture.

This approach considers all the references to the word or topic and identifies what scripture teaches in each passage. This learning is then assembled, in a mosaic form, to create a more full understanding of that given topic.

Some common topics might be:

- Love
- Grace
- Forgiveness

Topical studies strive to rightly handle God's word. So it is crucial that for each passage being considered, the student must take the time to understand the author, audience and the context of the passage. Only in doing this can we properly understand what the author is trying to communicate, and gain the correct understanding.

Once a topical study has been completed, the student will have a very detailed understanding of the word or topic. However this understanding must be handled correctly. It cannot be simply injected into any passage that references the topic. Once again, context will be used to determine which aspects of the meaning are appropriate.

Systematic study

OLOGY = The study of...

Theology Proper: God the Father
Bibliology: the Bible
Christology: Jesus Christ
Pneumatology: the Holy Spirit
Anthropology: Man/humanity
Hamartiology: Sin
Soteriology: Salvation
Ecclesiology: the Church
Angelology: Angels
Satanology: Satan
Demonology: Demons
Eschatology: End times

The systematic study topics are often called "doctrines" and represent the foundational truth statements of the Christian faith.

Systematic theology breaks God's word into different topics and identifies the truth about those topics. It also defines how those topics relate to each other. The primary focus here is around organizing knowledge and truth into unambiguous statements. In many ways it brings a scientific-like discipline to studying what God has to say.

A systematic study is like a word or topical study in that it uses the entire Bible to develop the truth-statements about each of the systematic topics. In the same way, systematic study must continue to understand the author, audience and context to establish the meaning of what is being said in each referenced passage. For this reason, learning textual study is critical to understanding a systematic study.

The Bible impacts your life right now!

If the Bible is the word of God, then it must continually impact our lives and the way we live.

Which of the study methods above have you begun to use, used regularly, mastered?

_____

What distractions lead you away from studying the Bible?

_____

_____

What lies do you believe that lead you away from time studying the Bible?

_____

_____

What one bold change do you need to make in your approach to studying the Bible?

_____

_____

03
Foundations of Textual Study (Part 1)

Tools to help you understand what the passage is trying to say

03 Foundations of Textual Study (Part 1)

Understanding the Big Picture

Author

What do we know about the person who wrote this?

Audience

What do we know about the recipients

Literature Style

What does the style of literature say?

The beginning of every Bible study is understanding the big picture.

The Bible doesn't exist in a vacuum. It always comes with context and a very specific setting. This has a tremendous impact on our overall understanding of any given passage.

Who wrote it? To whom were they writing? What style of writing did they use? These are critical opening questions for the Bible student. And despite how you might feel about these questions now, they can be answered relatively easily and will deliver a great insight on any passage.

The beginning of any Bible study is generally to take a step back and consider the big picture before diving into the details. Typically this means reviewing the entire book of the Bible to obtain the correct context for the passage of interest.

Discover the author

The first task of any Bible student is to understand what the author communicated to their audience.

Begin by identifying the author. Who were they? What do we know about them, and how does it give us insight into what they are saying? What is their status, position, role? What kinds of topics or issues do they want to address? Is there something that they want to accomplish that we should bear in mind?

The author is the first critical piece to being able to understand what God has to say to us.

Following is a short list of different books of the Bible. List out what is known about the author and how it can affect your study.

Genesis:

_____

Judges:

_____

Psalms:

_____

Isaiah:

_____

John:

_____

Ephesians:

_____

2 Peter:

_____

Identify the audience

To whom was this written? The identity of the audience gives invaluable clues to the meaning of the passage.

Often the passage, or the larger book, will provide clues about the initial readers of the message. What do we know about them, their relationship to the author, the specific circumstances they were facing, and their relationship to God?

If the audience is a troubled church, we'd expect one kind of message. If the audience is the rebellious nation of Israel, we would expect something different. Discover the audience as a clue to what God is trying to say.

Following is a short list of different books of the Bible. List out what is known about the initial readers and how it can affect your study.

Genesis:

_____

Judges:

_____

Psalms:

_____

Isaiah:

_____

John:

_____

Ephesians:

_____

2 Peter:

_____

Genres of Literature

History

Tells a story of what happened. Can be objective, or a first-hand perspective. Tends to focus on a general, not specific, audience. Is more focused on background and education.

Gospels

Similar to history in that it tells a story, but in this case the subject of the story is Jesus' life and death. Gospel literature points directly to salvation.

Poetry

Uses picturesque language to communicate feelings or an internal state. Tends to be more personal than educational

Prophecy

Communication coming directly from God. Often involving events which have not yes happened. Often based on imagery or graphic word pictures.

Letters

Letters written from one person to another, or a specific group. Can be both educational and teaching, or very personal depending on the author's message.

Wisdom

An ancient form of literature that focused on communicating wise teaching through a specific format and pattern of writing.

What type of literature?

A poem is different from a letter which is different from an historical account.

Different authors use different genres or styles of literature to communicate their message. This choice is just as important as the specific words they choose to use. Sometimes the purpose of the book itself determines the genre. Other times the specific message is best communicated in a certain style.

Sometimes, different books of the bible will employ different literary styles or conventions within a given book (poetic outburst, parable, genealogy...). Even these changes provide clues to what the author is trying to say.

Following is a short list of different books of the Bible. List out what is known about the type of literature and how it can affect your study.

Genesis:

_____

Judges:

_____

Psalms:

_____

Isaiah:

_____

John:

_____

Ephesians:

_____

2 Peter:

_____

You took me out of context!

Modern communication is characterized by behaviors that work against a proper understanding of the Bible.

These skills and behaviors are commonly used by many people as techniques for managing the onslaught of information in our society today. They are largely aimed at filtering out information we don't need to pay attention to.

However, when reading and studying, the Bible we need less filtering, not more filtering. So it is important for the Bible student to avoid these techniques.

Skimming:

_____

Partial Reading:

_____

Sound bites:

_____

Multi-tasking:

_____

Bible study reading skills

Studying God's Word requires an approach which ensures the correct context is set and the proper message is received.

The Bible student must develop new skills and techniques to properly handle God's word. These skills are focused on deep comprehension and focus. They help us tune out distractions which would otherwise interfere with our understanding.

At first, these techniques might seem strange and unfamiliar. With repetition and practice, they will become more comfortable.

Deep reading:

_____

_____

Reading through:

_____

_____

Finding context:

_____

_____

Dedicated focus:

_____

_____

It's all about the context

Every time we study the Bible, the passage must be understood in the context of how it was being communicated by the author to the audience.

"A young believer looking for wisdom in a difficult circumstance opened their bible at random and picked a verse to read: Matthew 27:5b. Shocked they opened to another random verse: Luke 10:37b. Completely shaken they tried one more time: John 13:27b."

Did this experience yield "rightly handling the word of truth"?

_____

_____

Read Luke 5:17-26

What do we know about the context?

_____

_____

_____

How does context help us understand the Pharisee's charge?

_____

_____

How does context help us understand Jesus' response?

_____

_____

The Bible impacts your life right now!

How are you tempted to short change your study of the word of God?

"Because I'm not skilled, I won't even try."

_____

"Because I don't have a lot of time, I won't use good technique."

_____

"I only want to study if I get feel-good messages in return."

_____

"I only want to study on my own terms."

_____

"I only want to study so I can get head-smart."

_____

Something else?

_____

04
Foundations of Textual Study (Part 2)

Understand how grammar impacts the meaning of the passage

04 Foundations of Textual Study (Part 2)

Using the tools of literature

Paragraphs

Contain one key thought or idea which is supported by several sentences.

Sentences

Come in different kinds which can be used to create different meanings.

Words

Key words can unlock meaning and show us what the author wanted to say.

Because the Bible is delivered to us as literature, we must use the fundamental tools of literature to discover what it means: Paragraphs, Sentences & Words.

As adults we generally understand the written word. But when it comes to studying the bible, it is useful to extend our normal comprehension so we can dig deeper and understand more of what God has to say.

The necessary tools are not difficult, we were probably taught most of what we need in middle school or Jr. High. But the odds are we haven't practiced these skills for a long time. They are there, but rusty.

Studying the Bible benefits the most from practice. Using the skills and tools over and over makes them much easier to use. Don't let the initial unfamiliarity prevent you from getting started.

Paragraphs as building blocks

When translating into English, most translators apply standard conventions of English grammar – including the use of paragraphs – even though they do not exist in the original manuscripts. This helps English readers properly understand what has been written.

A paragraph consists of several sentences that are grouped together. This group of sentences together discuss one main subject. In U.S. formal academic English, paragraphs have three principal parts. These three parts are the topic sentence, body sentences, and the concluding sentence.
http://lrs.ed.uiuc.edu/students/fwalt ers/para.html

When you encounter a paragraph in the biblical text, *it is appropriate to identify the main subject.* What is the paragraph about?

- The paragraph may not lead with the topic sentence, so you may need to search for it.
- The topic may be implied or pointed to, but not explicitly stated.

Once you have identified the subject of the paragraph, you have a good idea what he author was trying to communicate. Each of the sentences should then relate to or support the main idea in some way or another.

Paragraphs are great building blocks of comprehension. In a larger passage, paragraphs are a great way to break down what has been written into more understandable chunks.

Identifying paragraph points

Test your understanding of paragraphs with this exercise. Don't worry about finding the "right answer". This is more about practicing how you understand paragraphs.

People who worry about finding the "right answer" tend to freeze up on exercises like this. Let the text itself guide you to the answer and you will find good answers.

Read Acts 6:1-6 and answer the questions below

What is the topic sentence?

_____

_____

What are the supporting or body sentences?

_____

_____

_____

What is the concluding sentence or result?

_____

_____

_____

Different kinds of sentences

Declarative: Makes a statement. This is a declarative sentence.

Genesis 1:1

_____

_____

Interrogative: Asks a question.

John 6:42:

_____

_____

Romans 6:1

_____

_____

In some cases the question asked presumes an answer. In the John passage above, the question is rhetorical in the affirmative. The Romans passage is a setup for an emphatic negative answer.

Not all sentences are created alike. Sentences can have very different structures – which results in very different kinds of meaning.

Different kinds of sentences

Just about every sentence you encounter will fall into one of these 4 types. You can use the sentence types to help you zero in on meaning.

Imperative: Gives a command or makes a request. Common in dialog, but can be used in other settings. Imperative statements should really grab our attention because they call for action from the reader.
Joshua 1:6:

_____

Romans 12:1-2

_____

_____

Exclamatory: Expresses strong feeling, emotion or opinion. Exclamatory sentences add emphasis to the point being made.
Psalm 23:1

_____

1 John 3:1

_____

Using sentences in Bible study

There is no limit to the ways different types of sentences are used in the Bible. The attentive student will, however, begin to identify patterns that aid in determining meaning.

When reading the epistles (letters in the New Testament), it is common to look for imperative sentences which issue commands that must be obeyed. Finding a commend in the middle of a long paragraph can bring focus to a passage which is otherwise confusing. A common practice is to highlight imperative sentences in a passage to help focus on the areas that demand special action.

Another common Bible study technique is to look for questions and answers. In dialog, these are often important interactions. In more narrative styles, these are the kinds of conventions that point to key messages in the text.

Exclamations are also a hint that something important is happening. They show emotion and intensity on the part of the author or speaker. Being able to identify these sentences can often lead to the emotional point of what is being said.

A look at grammar and structures

Since Biblical communication is made of words, their meaning and structure have a significant impact on the message being sent.

You are encouraged to become familiar with words which tend to be associated with key points or meanings in the text of a given passage. These words are common ones across the English language and create a direct method to identify where key points are being made.

Often Bible study is about identifying where conclusions are being drawn or where contrasts are being made. In these places you can more easily focus on the point the author was making.

In general, this technique focuses on the connecting words in the English language. These connecting words are used to link sentences together in logical ways – and it is this logical linking that reveals what is being communicated.

The most common connections are **summarization**, **conclusion** and **contrast**.

Summarization shows where the author is distilling the essence of previous points in a concise format. In conclusion statements, the author brings together several ideas and provides the logical outcome of the ideas. In contrast, two ore more ideas are compared and shown to be different or opposite.

Conjunctions as linking words

AND – More of the same

Matthew 6:11-13:

_____

_____

_____

BUT – Contrast; the opposite

Romans 12:2

_____

_____

_____

Conjunctions are words which link together multiple complete ideas. They focus on a specific kind of additive or contrasting relationship between the ideas.

Prepositions as linking words

A preposition describes a relationship between other words in a sentence. Typically the preposition links a major idea (independent clause) with a secondary idea (dependent clause).

BECAUSE – for the reason that; what follows is a consequence of what precedes, linking

Ephesians 2:4-5

_____

_____

_____

FOR – Indicate purpose/goal; with respect to; because, why

Ephesians 2:8-10

_____

_____

_____

Other words that bear noting

THEREFORE – Consequence of what came before

Hebrews 12:1

_____

_____

_____

The same applies to other variants of this word such as wherefore. Therefore always drives you back to the what came before. It may be referring to a single sentence, or to the contents of an entire chapter (or more!) that was written previously.

REPETITION – Using a word over and over throughout a passage

John:15:1-11

_____

_____

When you encounter a "therefore" in the text, ask "Wherefore is the therefore there for?" In other words, stop and take note of the word and identify what it is trying to communicate.

The Bible impacts your life right now!

How are you tempted to short change your study of the word of God?

Studying God's Word means getting into a level of details. What would hinder you from doing this?

_____

_____

A few tools were illustrated in this lesson; what would prevent you from learning more tools (e.g. grammar) so that you could better study God's word?

_____

_____

What rewards could you receive for pursuing this kind of detail in studying God's word?

_____

_____

05
Applying What You Learn

The study is incomplete until you apply it to your life

05 Applying What We Learn

Simply understanding is not enough

The purpose of studying the Bible begins with understanding what the author is saying to their audience, but it does not stop there!

Understand what God is saying (comprehension) + Apply it to my life (application) Yields Grow & be transformed (transformation)

Studying the Bible without applying it will not result in the proper transformation and growth (milk to meat) that God intended. The different parts of this process are neither more nor less important that the others. What is important is that the ENTIRE process be completed to produce the correct result.

Proper application goes through a regular and repeatable set of steps:

Message Identification – what was the author trying to communicate to the original audience?

Audience mapping – how much is the original audience like me?

Message mapping – which elements of the message are relevant to me?

Action planning – what do I need to do in response?

Identify the message

The last few lessons in this study have been focused on identifying the message. We have been over several techniques and tools such as:

- Author identification
- Audience identification
- Type of literature that is being used
- Establishing a context and working within that context

In addition we have focused on tools which allow us to identify the actual message in a passage

- Paragraphs as containing a single main idea
- Sentences has having different types and purposes
- Key words that help reveal meaning.

The message is defined as what the original author communicated to the original readers.

These tools are designed to help us complete this first step in the application process. This step will probably take the bulk of the time of our study. Once the message has been identified, the rest of the application process can move forward.

Mapping the audience

Key Principle: Identify how the original audience is like me (culturally, temporally, spiritually, etc.).

Leviticus 16:1-10

_____

_____

Psalms 1:1-2

_____

_____

Matthew 4:12-17

_____

_____

John 3:16

_____

_____

Galatians 5: 16-24

_____

_____

Mapping the message

If the original audience is very distant from me, I can apply general principles. Some examples might include:

- What does the passage say about God, His character, His values and His plan?
- What does the people say about people in general, or the "human condition"?
- What are the characteristics of the way God relates to the people that are relevant today?

If the original audience is very similar to me, I can apply specific messages. Some examples might include:

- What actions does the passage call me to take?
- What does the passage forbid?
- How does the passage tell me I should behave?
- How does this passage exemplify the gospel?

If the original audience is neither distant nor similar, I can apply general principles and some specific messages.

- Any message that is specific to a way that the original audience is different than me cannot be applied directly
- Any general principle that is always true can still be applied

Mapping the message

Key Principle: The more the audience is like me, the more directly God's message applies.

Leviticus 16:1-10

Psalms 1:1-2

Matthew 4:12-17

John 3:16

Galatians 5: 16-24

Plan for action

James 1:22-25

We are called to take action based on what we
see in God's word.

Philippians 3:12-16

We press forward toward Jesus.

Philippians 1:3-11

It is Jesus (through the Holy Spirit) who
produces the change.

Key Principle:
Where God
commands, I must
obey. Where God
forbids, I must
avoid. What God
likes, I must like.
What God hates, I
must hate.

The Bible impacts your life right now!

Do you let God's word have an impact in your life? Or do you make it stop at your head? The longest journey is often the 18 inches from your head to your heart!

What is the percentage of energy you spend identifying the meaning of a passage vs. applying it to your life? Is that the right split?

_____

_____

When you find an application, do you take it to heart, or just brush it off as inconsequential?_____

_____

After you study the Bible, how much energy do you spend trying to take action on what has been applied?

_____

_____

_____

06
Using Resources Wisely

Choosing the right resource can make a difference in your study

06 Using Resources Wisely

It's not a race to the answer

When studying the Bible, it's important to get a correct answer. But that does not mean you should simply go read what someone else has determined for the passage you're studying.

One of the key benefits of studying the Bible is the study process itself. It may seem difficult and confusing and you might not get to an answer as quickly as you want. That's ok. The process of wrestling with God's word will pay dividends in your life.

The application you make will be many times more impactful if it represents work and effort to arrive at it. So don't think that you are wasting your time. You're not!!

Skill in studying the Bible comes with practice. And that means continuing to study even when you just want to get to the answer of "what should I do

If you lack confidence in your conclusions and applications, that's normal and to be expected. Keep doing what you're doing, but find a Bible study partner where you can share your findings with them and discuss how they could be improved or corrected. It's ideal if that person is a little more experienced than you are – then they can provide tips and hints along the way.

Whatever you do, don't fall into the trap of looking up the answer in an external resource because you are not comfortable studying for yourself.

Resources are not a crutch

Today's Bible student has more resources at their disposal than did many scholars several centuries ago. But not all resources are good for the beginning student. Resources have a specific place in the Bible study process, and can be a great assist when used within those parameters.

2 Timothy 2:15 (a)

- Be diligent to present yourself approved to God (NASB)
- Study to shew thyself approved unto God (KJV)
- Do your best to present yourself to God as one approved (ESV)
- Work hard so you can present yourself to God and receive his approval (NLT)

What image or sense does this text evoke?

_____

_____

It is a proper biblical expectation that studying will take effort and energy and time. Only with much practice will it *appear* to be "easy". But for that student, the difficulty will have just moved to another level and new challenges will preset as old challenges are overcome.

How to approach studying the Bible

Resources are used to answer specific questions that arise out of the text which we cannot answer with our personal knowledge.

- When was this written?
- What does that word mean?
- Who is that person and what did they do?
- What is the audience's greatest need?
- What else was going on when this was written?

1, Read the text: Establish author, audience and context

2. Read the text: Identify the message being communicated

3. Identify questions that you want to have answered: Use resources to find answers.

"What does this mean?" is not a legitimate question. Questions are intended to help you so that YOU can identify what the passage is about and what it means.

4. Read the text: Identify the message being communicated

5. Map the audience & message: Apply the message to your life

6. Compare your conclusions with others: Trace back any differences to the text

Resource 1: Paper and Pen

Believe it or not, your eyes and a pen or pencil are the most important resource you'll find!

Get a fresh look at the passage by copying it into your favorite word processing application. Use the formatting to give it wide margins and generous spacing. Then read over it a few times to get the sense of what is being said. Use paragraph format so you can group together the main ideas and supporting text.

Then use a pen or pencil to note questions that occur to you while you are reading. Just put them in the margin. Highlight important or repeated words. Sometimes they will show a pattern throughout the text.

Sometimes it's helpful to get the text out of your Bible. Many Bibles today have small print and cramped margins, so there is a very limited opportunity to be able to put your thoughts and questions on the page.

As you learn more about the passage, jot this down too! When you are done, this printed copy will become an invaluable resource of information on the passage,. Not only that, but all your notes will remind you of the learning and discovery process you followed to be able to come to some conclusions.

It can be very beneficial to go back and look at old study notes and see how much you've learned and recall the discover process again.

Resource 2: Study Bible

Suggested Options:

ESV Study Bible

Ryrie Study Bible

John MacArthur Study Bible

NIV Zondervan Study Bible

Study Bibles are chock-full of useful resources that can really help.

A good study bible is a treasure trove of useful resources. Whether you are looking for help on a specific passage, or if you want to expand your knowledge of Bible study, your Study Bible will have a great set of tools for taking you deeper.

- Cross- references
- Maps & Diagrams
- Book overviews/introductions
- Resource materials
- Cross Reference Notes
- Notes, explanations & commentary **

Take some time to review all the reference materials that are available in your study Bible. Don't just look within the text of the scripture. Most study Bibles have significant materials at the end or beginning too.

Resource 3: Bible Dictionary

A Bible dictionary offers an alphabetized list of words with definitions and explanations.

A Bile dictionary won't explain the meaning of a given passage of scripture, but it will give you background on may of the things you read about in your Bible. A Bible dictionary is a useful resource when trying to answer questions that arise out of reading the path. You will find that the dictionary has useful background and explanatory information on may different people, places, events and objects.

Do you want a brief biography of Naaman? An overview of the Galilee region of Israel? A summary of the Babylonian conquest of Jerusalem? Or perhaps an explanation of what is a synagogue? A Bible dictionary will have entries on all these items that will provide you with a brief background and overview so you can better understand them as they occur in the passage.

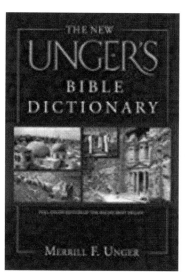

Recommended

Resource 4: Bible Handbook

Recommended

A Bible handbook offers an background and insight into passages of scripture.

A Bible handbook is similar to a Bible dictionary, except in stead of being organized alphabetically by topic, it is organized by the order of passages in the Bible. The Bible Handbook will provide a significant amount of information to introduce each of the 66 books (similar to your study bible, but perhaps in more detail), Additionally the handbook will offer background regarding different paragraphs in the passage itself.

It would be interesting to think that the Bible handbook provides the entire study for a given passage in the Bible. However the real purpose is to gain insight into what the passage is talking about so that you can draw your own conclusions based on what the text says, rather than what the handbook says.

Resource 5: Theology & Doctrine

A systematic theology book provides you with in-depth topical information about the various doctrines of the Christian faith.

As you encounter different topics throughout your study, you might want to know more about their theological and doctrinal perspectives. A book of Systematic Theology presents these materials in an effective way to understand what we believe on the topic and how it relates to other topics and doctrines.

A book of theology and doctrine is a tremendous resource as you dig into different theological topics. Not only will it address the scope of the theology, but also variations and their origins, as well as discussions of different considerations and angles to consider. A good Systematic Theology will be loaded with scriptural references so you can link the material back to what God actually says.

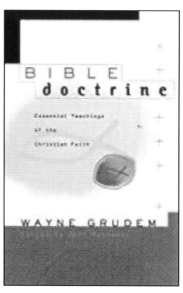

Recommended

The internet is NOT a resource

Several Bible-based websites can be very useful and have been proven trustworthy over time.

Blue Letter Bible
blb.org

Bible Gateway
biblegateway.com

Logos Bible Software
logos.com

While the internet is tempting and easy to access, it is the breeding ground of heresy, ignorance, misinformation and bad theology.

The internet is full of people you do not know, who have not been verified or validated. Their theology and teaching has not been tested and found to be good. You do not know whether you are getting truth or lies from them. Assume lies.

While it may be tempting to use a search engine to look for information on the internet, this is not a valid study technique. All of the materials recommended in this course have been reviewed and found to be trustworthy. The same cannot be said of resources found on the internet.

Unless you receive a recommendation from a mature believer, you should be skeptical about anything you find there.

The Bible impacts your life right now!

Consider the recommendations above; how many of them have you violated while trying to study God's word previously? Will you commit to change?

_____

_____

Do you have a good set of resources at home that will support an effective study of the Bible? Will you commit to expand your resources?

_____

_____

A 6-step approach to bible study was laid out. Will you commit to using it to study a passage of the bible in the next 2 weeks?

_____

_____

Do you use resources properly or are they a shortcut to an easy answer that avoids the work of digging in yourself?

Next Steps

Where will you go from here?

Congratulations on completing the materials in this course!

This brings you to a new beginning, not an end. The information in this course is designed to prepare you for actually studying the Bible .

So it's time to begin using this material to **actually study the Bible!**

Practice is the most essential ingredient for effective Bible study.

If you don't begin using what you've learned, you will start to forget all of it.

When you do start to use it, it will feel awkward and difficult. That's normal for any new skill, so don't get upset about it. This is new and you're not used to it. Practice is the only way it will begin to feel normal.

Your challenge is to start studying the Bible NOW.

- Pick something that interests you.
- Pick something reasonably sized.
- Pick a partner to do it with and keep you accountable.

What you do next is up to you. There is no easy way to get ahead. Digging in is the only path. Don't wait any longer.

Take the next step!

07
Introduction to Titus

Get prepared for your first Bible study

07 Introduction to Titus

Titus is a great starter-study

Fast Facts about Titus:

Author: Paul

Audience: Titus

Chapters: 3

Timeline: 1st Century

Topics: Christian living in a time of false teachers.

The next step in this workbook is a study of the book of Titus.

You might not be familiar with this book of the Bible. That's OK. When you're done, you will be! Titus is a great starter study for a number of reasons:

1. **It's Short**. When starting out, it's best to take an easy first step. Length of the book is one of the factors that adds difficulty to a study.

2. **It's written to an individual**. Some books of the Bible have an ambiguous audience. Or they are written to a group of people. Titus is written to a church leader named Titus. This helps keep it more focused.

3. **It's simple and practical**. Paul has a few direct points to make. This makes understanding easier.

Create Your Study Text

You are free to use a copy of your Bible as a study manuscript. However, it can be useful to make a copy of the text for studying.

Throughout the study you might want to mark up the text with margin notes and marks on words to highlight frequency or key points. Your Bible probably doesn't have enough space for these things.

You will also want a text which is free of notes that might move you out of sequence in the study process.

Creating your own copy in a work processor. Copy and paste the text out of one of the online resources from Session 6.

Formatting your manuscript:

Margins: At least 1.5" on all four sides.

Spacing: Double

Remember to add page numbers

Leave chapter and verse markers

Edit out other notes and links

Hint: When pasting use Paste Special and choose Plain Text.

What do you learn about the Author?

Read the entire book of Titus and note everything the author reveals about himself.

If you created a study manuscript, use a pen or colored pencils to highlight the sections.

What do you learn about the Author?

_____

_____

_____

_____

_____

_____

_____

_____

_____

_____

What do you learn about the Audience?

What do you learn about the Audience?

_____

_____

_____

_____

_____

_____

_____

_____

_____

_____

Read the entire book of Titus and note everything the author reveals about his audience.

If you created a study manuscript, use a pen or colored pencils to highlight the sections.

What are the key words in the text?

Read the entire book of Titus and note any key words that seem to have special importance.

If you created a study manuscript, use a pen or colored pencils to mark the words so they are more visible.

When marking a manuscript, it's helpful to make a key so you know what words or concepts you're tracking and how they are marked. Write down the word and mark it how it will be identified in the text.

Key Words

———————————

———————————

———————————

———————————

———————————

———————————

———————————

———————————

———————————

Summarize the paragraphs

Since Titus is such a short book, paragraphs make meaningful building blocks

In longer books you could use other structural units such as entire chapters. In the ESV translation, there are eight paragraphs in the book. So come up with a summary for each one.

A paragraph summary is a special technique. When we looked at paragraphs in Chapter Four we said that every paragraph has a theme sentence. When you summarize the paragraph, you'll want to identify that theme and represent it in one or two key words, ideally taken from the sentence itself.

By summarizing paragraphs, we'll gain a birds-eye view of the entire book. The message of the book is the sum of the messages of the paragraphs.. In twenty words or less, you'll have a quick overview.

Paragraph Summary

_____

_____

_____

_____

_____

_____

_____

_____

_____

Write down any questions

As you read the book, you might uncover some questions.

By writing them down , you'll free up your brain to leave them alone for a while,.

If you're ready with some resources, you can start to do some research now. Try to limit your research to only answer the questions lest you start to get biased by outside influences..

Overview Questions

_____

_____

_____

_____

_____

_____

_____

_____

_____

Summarize Titus

What Titus is about:

_____

_____

_____

_____

_____

_____

_____

_____

Summarize

Write out a short overview of the book of Titus. You should include the results of each of the steps that you've just gone through.

Author, Audience, Keywords, Paragraph and any of your questions.

The summary doesn't have to be in pretty sentences. But it should represent what you've learned about the book.

08
Titus Chapter 1

Digging into God's word, one chapter at a time.

08 Titus Chapter 1

Getting ready for a chapter study

Get ready by reviewing your notes

Go back over your notes from Session Seven. Look at the message for the entire book and note what parts of that message are associated with Chapter One.

Take a moment to review your manuscript and see if you marked any keywords or other observations that will help you dig deeper into the chapter.

Now you're ready to dig into the Six-Step study process!

1. Read the text and identify Author, Audience, Context

2. Read the Text and identify the Author's message

3. Identify questions you want to answer.

4. Read the text and refine the Author's message

5. Map the Audience and message

6. Compare your conclusions with others

In the last lesson, you completed step one. Going forward you'll look back at Lesson Seven for that. This time around you'll start with step two.

Identify the Chapter One Message

Chapter One is about:

_____

_____

_____

_____

_____

_____

_____

_____

_____

Read over Chapter One and identify the author's message.

Look at the paragraph summaries, keywords you've highlighted, and any notes you've already made.

Think about Paul trying to communicate to Timothy and how he might have wanted to approach the topics in this chapter.

You might even spend some time looking for new patterns in words or ideas.

List out your questions and research

As you review Titus chapter one for the message you'll probably stumble across some questions. Write them down and move on.

When you're ready, return to the questions and use some of your resources to see if you can find answer to the questions.

Ideally, answering the questions will help you understand the message of chapter one more clearly.

Chapter One Questions & Answers:

_____

_____

_____

_____

_____

_____

_____

_____

_____

Refine the Chapter One Message

Chapter One Message Refined:

_____

_____

_____

_____

_____

_____

_____

_____

Now that you know more...

Go back to chapter one and review what you've written down about the message of the chapter.

Use the information you learned from your research to refine that and refine your understanding of the message.

Map the Audience

Titus is both like us and different from us.

You will use these similarities and differences to understand how to apply Paul's message to your own life.

No Bible audience is ever 100% identical to us today. There are always small difference that can influence how we apply the message to our own lives.

To the extent Titus is like us, we can directly apply Paul's message.

Similarities might relate to his understanding of the Gospel or this role in life or in the church.

To the extent Titus is different from us we have to generalize Paul's message.

Some difference don't matter. Other differences can cause you to shift your application a lot.

Titus is similar:

_____

_____

_____

_____

Titus is Different:

_____

_____

_____

_____

Map the Message

Chapter One Message Mapped:

_____

_____

_____

_____

_____

_____

_____

_____

_____

Some questions you might consider as you map are:

1. What commands must you obey?

2. What Truth must you hold dear?

3. What error must your run away from?.

4. How is God revealed in this text?

5. How is the gospel made clear?

Make an Action Plan

Unless the Bible changes your life, it's not doing you any good.

So make an action plan based on the message of the chapter.

What do you need to start doing because of what the chapter says? What should you stop? How will you know that the change is real in your life?

Titus Chapter One Action Plan:

_____

_____

_____

_____

_____

_____

_____

_____

09
Titus Chapter 2

A deeper look at Titus chapter two

09 Titus Chapter 2

Identify the Chapter Two Message

Read over chapter two and identify the author's message.

Look at the paragraph summaries, keywords you've highlighted, and any notes you've already made.

Think about Paul trying to communicate to Timothy and how he might have wanted to approach the topics in this chapter.

You might even spend some time looking for new patterns in words or ideas.

Chapter Two Is About:

_____

_____

_____

_____

_____

_____

_____

_____

List out your questions and research

Chapter Two Questions & Answers:

_____

_____

_____

_____

_____

_____

_____

_____

As you review Titus chapter two for the message you'll probably stumble across some questions. Write them down and move on.

When you're ready, return to the questions and use some of your resources to see if you can find answer to the questions.

Ideally, answering the questions will help you understand the message of chapter two more clearly.

Refine the Chapter Two Message

Now that you know more...

Go back to chapter two and review what you've written down about the message of the chapter.

Use the information you learned from your research to refine that and refine your understanding of the message.

Chapter Two Message Refined:

_____

_____

_____

_____

_____

_____

_____

_____

Map the Audience

You've already mapped Titus once.

As you go through subsequent chapters, you will mostly need to review your previous mapping to see if something has changed.

Throughout the letter, Paul may address different aspects of Titus' role. In one place he may be speaking to Titus the Pastor. In another place he might be talking to Titus the Believer. These would reasonably map differently to you today.

Once you've mapped the audience you just need to keep track of how the audience is being addressed so you can apply the correct message mapping.

Titus is similar:

_____

_____

_____

_____

Titus is Different:

_____

_____

_____

_____

Map the Message

Some questions you might consider as you map are:

1. What commands must you obey?

2. What Truth must you hold dear?

3. What error must your run away from?.

4. How is God revealed in this text?

5. How is the gospel made clear?

Chapter Two Message Mapped:

_____

_____

_____

_____

_____

_____

_____

_____

Make an Action Plan

Titus Chapter Two Action Plan:

_____

_____

_____

_____

_____

_____

_____

_____

Unless the Bible changes your life, it's not doing you any good.

So make an action plan based on the message of the chapter.

What do you need to start doing because of what the chapter says? What should you stop? How will you know that the change is real in your life?

10
Titus Chapter 3

Finishing up Titus by studying chapter three

10 Titus Chapter 3

Identify the Chapter Three Message

Read over chapter three and identify the author's message.

Look at the paragraph summaries, keywords you've highlighted, and any notes you've already made.

Think about Paul trying to communicate to Timothy and how he might have wanted to approach the topics in this chapter.

You might even spend some time looking for new patterns in words or ideas.

Chapter Three is about:

_____

_____

_____

_____

_____

_____

_____

_____

List out your questions and research

Chapter Three Questions & Answers:

_____

_____

_____

_____

_____

_____

_____

_____

_____

As you review Titus chapter three for the message you'll probably stumble across some questions. Write them down and move on.

When you're ready, return to the questions and use some of your resources to see if you can find answer to the questions.

Ideally, answering the questions will help you understand the message of chapter three more clearly.

Refine the Chapter Three Message

Now that you know more...

Go back to chapter three and review what you've written down about the message of the chapter.

Use the information you learned from your research to refine that and refine your understanding of the message.

Chapter Three Message Refined:

_____

_____

_____

_____

_____

_____

_____

Map the Audience

You've already mapped Titus.

As you go through subsequent chapters, you will mostly need to review your previous mapping to see if something has changed.

Throughout the letter, Paul may address different aspects of Titus' role. In one place he may be speaking to Titus the Pastor. In another place he might be talking to Titus the Believer. These would reasonably map differently to you today.

Once you've mapped the audience you just need to keep track of how the audience is being addressed so you can apply the correct message mapping.

Titus is similar:

_____

_____

_____

Titus is Different:

_____

_____

_____

Map the Message

Some questions you might consider as you map are:

1. What commands must you obey?

2. What Truth must you hold dear?

3. What error must your run away from?.

4. How is God revealed in this text?

5. How is the gospel made clear?

Chapter Three Message Mapped:

_____

_____

_____

_____

_____

_____

_____

_____

_____

Make an Action Plan

Titus Chapter Three Action Plan:

_____

_____

_____

_____

_____

_____

_____

_____

_____

Unless the Bible changes your life, it's not doing you any good.

So make an action plan based on the message of the chapter.

What do you need to start doing because of what the chapter says? What should you stop? How will you know that the change is real in your life?

Congratulations!

Now you've completed the entire course. You've learned how to study your Bible and you've done your first study. Now it's time to start your next one!

Don't let time slip way before you reinforce what you've just learned. What would you like to study next?

Let me know at Dennis@Dennis-Stevenson.com

Printed in Great Britain
by Amazon